How to use your teeth until 100 years old

This book is dedicated to people all over the world who like to protect their teeth

如何讓牙齒使用到 100 歲

這本書獻給，全世界喜歡保護牙齒的人

This book can reduce the chances of you going to the dentist to cause illness. you will never regret it.

After reading this book, it is like giving you a valuable gift, you will never forget it for the rest of your life

The Chinese have a very simple method that can make humanity use their teeth until they are 100 years old. I hope that people all over the world will have this opportunity to learn this method. Let the teeth use to 100 years old and easy to improve everyone's quality of life.

中國老祖先的 5000 年智慧結晶 - 易經

The crystallization of 5000 years of wisdom of Chinese ancestors-Book of Changes (Please refer to P.59 in this book)

People all over the world come to study the Book of Changes, there is no nuclear war in the world

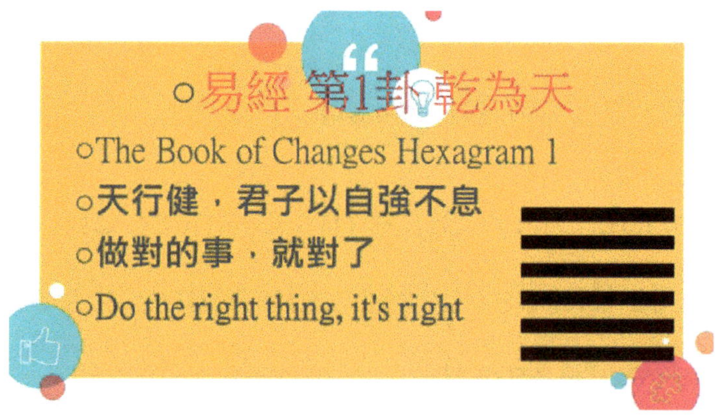

Protecting teeth is your own responsibility and right, just do it right

Title page

How to use your teeth until 100 years old

By: George Ho

This is human, dental care, the ultimate goal

If your dental care method is correct

Your teeth can be used up to 100 years old.

After massage your teeth can reduce your chances of going to the dentist for treatment, and you will never regret it.

ABSTRACT

Everyone cares about the health of their teeth. The way people care for their teeth is only brush their teeth, to keep their teeth clean, not to caries, and to have white teeth. Wrong, this is only 50 points. The ultimate goal of dental care is to keep the teeth from falling out and use it until you die. This is the 100-point protection concept for your teeth.

Most people think that when they are old, their teeth will fall off, & is a natural phenomenon. It is commonly called " When people are old, they will start to lose their teeth." However, This is a concern that has been wrong for many years. Western medicine & dentists have proven that If teeth are properly protected when young, they can theoretically last a lifetime. Just like you protect your knees, your knees are well protected and can be used for a lifetime. (Ref: Dr. Luo Shaorui, Director of Department of Orthopedics, Dalin Tzu Chi Hospital, Chiayi Hsien Taiwan. R.O.C). Therefore, as long as you understand the cause of the tooth loss and prevent the problem by reason, it is easier to prevent the tooth loss.

According to the World Health Organization (WHO) Please refer to P.72 of this book, 95% of the main causes of human tooth loss are caused by periodontal disease and dental caries. The remaining 5% are caused by accidental impact trauma. About 30% of the world's people of 65-74 years old do not have natural teeth, and natural teeth will completely fall off. It is everywhere, so the average person has serious tooth loss. If you don't do any prevention action. About a person will start to lose his teeth when he is 45 years old, and about one-half of his teeth at the age of 80 . The WHO only tells you that prevention of periodontal disease and dental caries can prevent 95% of the teeth from falling. But there is no practical simple way to teach you how to prevent tooth loss? This book teaches you what is the practical and simple way to protect your teeth. It is hoped that WHO can widely promote this concept to the whole world.

1500 years ago, the Chinese had already developed a set of methods to prevent tooth loss. The three methods of tooth care created by the Tang Dynasty' s medicine king Sun Simiao (A.D.557~682) were "interlock teeth, secrete salivation, and gingival massage" He also said, "When I get up in the morning, I interlock my teeth 36 times, but my teeth don't fall." In Taiwan, because of the decline of Chinese medicine and medical skills, the government attaches great importance to Western medicine and does not advocate Chinese medicine, so there are not many people who know the methods.

In addition, more earlier,Master Bodhidharma (A.D.382~540) Yi-jin-jing Book can prevent tooth loss. But most people don't know that there is this method in this world, because this method is private, oral, and taught by the master and apprentice. There is no written record, and the academic paper has not been proposed for discussion.

But to protect the teeth so that they do not fall out, some people in China have studied it about 1500 years ago and it can be successful. It's just that no one reported it in the official Western medical literature. (Because the history of Western medicine is only 392 years old. Please refer to P.29 of this book. There was no internet at that time.)

Therefore, this article introduces this method for the first time in academic papers to the medical community and the general public all over the world to discuss and awaken the attention of the world. Let the people of the world know. It can be successful to protect teeth from falling out, and it should be done at a young age, the sooner the better. Because young people have serious tooth decay, young people can also lose their teeth. Let people in the world know that there is a simple and cheap way to protect your teeth. I hope that people all over the world, no matter where you live on the earth, have a better understanding of the health care methods of teeth.

Whether you are a dentist or the general public, it is worthwhile to study and practice the method that this book teaches you. Because the method taught in this book is free, has no side effects, and can help clean teeth. This book can reduce your chances of going to the dentist for treatment.

In order to spread the world, the price is set at a low price, hoping to allow more people to benefit.

If you are blessed to be able to practice and complete the protection methods of this book, your life will become happier, fuller, healthier, and improve your quality of life. In any case, I hope that this book can bring healthier teeth to people all over the world. & a better earth.

Keywords : teeth , preventive medicine, Dental care, Sun Simiao , W.H.O Oral hygiene

摘要 (序文)

大家都很關心牙齒的健康，一般人保健牙齒的方法，只會刷牙，讓牙齒保持乾淨、不想蛀牙、及有潔白牙齒的目標而已。錯了，這只有 50 分。牙齒保健的終極目標，是讓牙齒永不脫落，牙齦穩固，到死之前都可使用它，這才是 100 分保護牙齒正確健康關念。

一般人都認為，年紀老了會掉牙齒，是自然現象，俗稱「老掉牙」，但是，這是一種存在多年錯誤的關念，西醫，牙醫師已經證明，如果牙齒保護得宜，牙齒理論上是可以使用一輩子的。這就像你保護腳膝蓋一樣，膝蓋保護得宜，是可以使用一輩子的。(請參閱；嘉義大林慈濟醫院 骨科主任 呂紹睿博士 YouTube 「膝蓋保護」法)。因此只要了解，掉牙齒的原因，由原因去預防問題，就可以更容易達到目標。

世界衛生組織 WHO 公告，人類會掉牙齒主要原因 95%是牙周病及齲齒(蛀牙)所造成，其餘 5%是意外撞擊外傷所引起，參閱本書 P.72 。全球約 30%的 65~74 歲人沒有自然牙齒，自然牙齒會出現完全脫落的現象，比比皆是，所以一般人，牙齒脫落現象很嚴重。如果你不做任何預防動作，大約人到 45 歲即會開始自然掉牙齒，80 歲時牙齒剩下約二分之一(2019 年台灣地區衛福部的統計)。WHO 只告訴你，預防牙周病及齲齒發生，即可預防 95%的掉牙。卻還沒有實際簡單方法，教你如何預防牙齒掉落? 本書即教你甚麼是實際簡單的方法。希望 WHO 能廣為推廣此觀念於全世界，拯救世人的牙齒。

1500 年前，中國人已有人，研發出來一套方法，可以預防牙齒掉落，唐朝的藥王 孫思邈(西元 557～682)所創牙齒保健方法「叩齒、漱津、揩齒」三招，並說「晨起叩齒 36 下，到老牙不落」，在台灣，因為中醫，醫術日道見微，政府重視西醫，不提倡中醫，所以知道此方法的人並不多。

另外，更早達摩祖師(西元 382～540)的易筋經，是有方法可以預防牙齒掉牙的。但大部份的人都不知道有這套方法，因為這套方法都是師徒私下，口傳，相授而已，不做文字記載。預防牙齒掉落，因此學術論文也尚未有人提出來討論。

但保護牙齒，讓牙齒不脫落，中國人約 1500 年前，已經有人研究出來，是可以成功的。只是沒人在正式西醫學文獻上報導 (因為西醫的歷史僅 392 年，請參閱本書 P.29，而那時候也沒有網路，知識的傳播很慢)。

所以本文首次以學術論文方式，介紹這套方法給全世界的醫學界及一般人士知道，並共同來討論，喚醒世人的注意，保護牙齒不脫落，是可以成功的，並應從年輕時開始做，愈早愈好。因為年輕人，齲齒嚴重，也可讓年輕人掉牙。本書讓世界的人，知道有這套簡單又省錢的方法，可以保護你的牙齒。希望全世界人類，不管你住在地球哪個地方，對牙齒的保健方法，有進一步的認識及瞭解。

不管你是誰，官員或是一般民眾，都值得你去研究實踐這本書教你的方法，因為你的一生都離不開牙齒，而這本書所教的方法是免費的、簡單的、沒有副作用，而且可以幫助潔牙(預防齲齒)。本書並可減少，你去找牙醫師治病的機會。

為了全面傳於世界，因此定價為銅板價，可讓更多的人得到受惠。

如果你有福氣能實踐並完成這本書的方法，你的人生會變得更愉快、更充實、更健康，並提高你的生活品質。無論如何，希望這本書，能帶來給全世界的人，更健康的牙齒，更美好的地球。

關鍵字: 牙齒、預防醫學、孫思邈、牙齒保健、W.H.O 口腔衛生

Introduction (簡介)

"When people are old, will to lose their teeth" is a misconception. This book lets people around the world know that teeth can be used for a lifetime. i-teeth Stick to Persist & Determining to practice this method, you will get unexpected results, because the book's method is free, and simple, & there are no side effects.

Readers share:

By Zhao Guixiang 2020.08.22

As soon as I got this book, I couldn’t wait to read it. I wanted to know the ways to protect my teeth from falling out. In the book, not only discussed the literature, collected specific suggestions from the dentist, but also provided you from a The Qi-gong Master learned a set of methods to protect the gums. I realized that massaging the gums is so important. I also tried to do this. Now I feel that the condition of my teeth has improved a lot. Thank you for sharing such good things. ~

THANKSGIVING

I am grateful that this life can meet the descendants of the Dharma ancestors, Professor Ren Shude, without his encounter, this book could not be completed. I am also grateful to Dr. Lin Zongzeng of National Kaohsiung University of Applied Sciences for his paper guidance, trained my skills in writing scientific papers, academic thinking logic, and some basic principles of being a human being. People have to live until they are old and learn to be old, especially the knowledge of a healthy body.

The human body is really too complicated. It is composed of tens of trillions of cells = $3.72*10^{13}$. The knowledge of physical health can never be carry out studied . But when people are old, they will know that to have a healthy body, you must start to act when you are young to pursue healthy goals, and the younger, the better. The same goes for tooth protection.

This book is written in the form of academic papers. I hope everyone can understand it more easily and participate in the discussion and research together. This book is also integrated with the dental health methods created by the Tang

Dynasty' s medicine king Sun Simiao, "interlock teeth, secrete salivation, and gingival massage" and the Yi-Jin-Jing Book of Master Bodhidharma plus my 27 years of accumulated experience in tooth protection. No matter who you are, you should actually try it out, because this method is free and simple. According to my actual case, through my practice and the experiments of many friends, it is proved that teeth can be used up to 100 years old is very easy. And it can reduce your chances of going to the dentist for treatment.

Accumulate my 27 years of practical experiments and the actual operation of some friends, this method proof is indeed helpful for some people to prevent ischemic periodontal disease and prevent the operation of tooth decay. So, it can prevent human teeth from falling. Therefore, I feel that I should give it to the world. I don't want to use only spoken words, only taught to a few people to know, so write this paper.

Anyway, seeing this paper. If you learn this method, learn it, and do it, you will earn it. It will never let you lose any time and waste time, and will help you reduce the chance of tooth decay, that is, have a function of cleaning teeth to make your teeth healthier.

I also want to thanks to the teacher of Yan Jean for his guidance and encouragement, this book can be successfully listed on the Amazon e-book platform.

Thanks to Freepik for providing free pictures of 6525. P.27 Image 1. Free pictures, Thanks to Tabitha Tumer from Unsplash for providing free picture, and Tanks to Photo Ac for providing free picture of 841688. Introduction to the inner page & on the cover.

Table of contents

Finally, please pay attention to e-book readers. Because e-books do not include the number of pages in ink, if you see the number of pages on the inside of the e-book, the number of pages refers to the number of pages in the paper book.

Chapter 1 Introduction The importance of teeth not falling off

Your teeth are forever, can't fall off, there are three reasons: 1. Don't have to spend money on dentures, dentures are never better than real teeth. 2. Eating three meals has a good taste, helps digestion, and prolongs your life. 3. Speaking will not leak, help you socialize

1.1 Don't have to spend money on dentures, dentures are never better than real teeth.

(First It is necessary to understand the cause of human tooth loss, so that the problem of tooth loss can be solved.)

According to the World Health Organization (WHO), 95% of the main causes of human tooth loss are caused by periodontal disease and dental caries. The remaining 5% are accidental impact injuries,That is to prevent periodontal disease and caries, can prevent 95% of teeth loss, but the dentist only tells you the reason, but there is no simple way how to prevent your teeth from falling. 1500 years ago, the Chinese already knew have a simple way to prevent teeth loss.

Because of the setting of human DNA, when human beings are 45 to 60 years old, the function of the body's five internal organs will gradually weaken, and the blood circulation function of the whole body will begin to slow down. Because the teeth are protected by the gums and functioning, the gums are gradually aging. The blood circulation of the gums is insufficient, Aging gums, the base of the tooth will start to loosen , causing gaps, the gums will begin to bleed, and the teeth will fall off naturally over time. (commonly known as: Ischemic Periodontal Disease) At this time, the effect of finding a dentist is not great. It is usually to stop bleeding and relieve pain. The dentist cannot prevent your gums from nature aging. If you do not take any preventive actions, 90% of them will not be spared, and you will start to lose teeth at the age of 45. On average, he loses all his teeth at the age of 70, and about one tooth is removed a year.

With a little change in physical fitness, some people will start to loosen when they are 40 years old, and almost 100% of them will fall to the remaining one-half when they are 80 years old (Statistics for National Health Service Taiwan Ministry of Health and Welfare in 2018.). Therefore, about 5% to 10% of people have teeth that can be used up to 100 years old.

There is one sentence "when people are old, they will lose their teeth" to remember and say, but this concern and statement is wrong. Western medicine & dentists have proved that If the teeth are properly protected when you are young, the teeth can theoretically be used for a lifetime. Just like you protect your knees, your knees are well protected and can be used for a lifetime. (Dr. Luo Shaorui, Director of Department of Orthopedics, Dalin Tzu Chi Hospital, Chiayi Hsien Taiwan R.O.C). https://dalin.tzuchi.com.tw/teampersonnel/348

Zhou Xinghua, associate professor of the School of Stomatology, Taipei Medical University, also said in the United Daily News on the 2019.5.12 report that "The course of periodontal disease is related to the tooth-cleaning habits, and is related to age and bone loss." Obviously, losing teeth has a lot to do with age.

People do not necessarily lose their teeth when they are old. About 5% to 10% of people will not lose their teeth. 90% of people will lose their teeth because they are old and the blood circulation function is reduced. The blood cannot reach the gums enough, and the gums will age. The dentist collectively says: "formation of ischemic periodontal disease." Therefore, as long as human beings pay attention to this situation, massage the gums to increase the blood circulation and transport function, so that the blood can fully reach the gums, can slow down the aging of the gums, and can prevent ischemic periodontal disease. In theory, it can prevent of tooth loss. Opportunity to fall. Therefore, the elderly lose their teeth, and dentists also call it a kind of periodontal disease.

Periodontal disease is basically defined as: a supporting tissue around the teeth, a disease that causes bacterial infection between the gums, commonly known as the muscles of the teeth, alveolar bone, and periodontal ligament. It causes damage to the periodontal tissue and then shakes, causing severe Causes tooth loss. The periodontal disease that dentists refer to is mainly divided into two categories:(1) gingivitis and (2) periodontitis.

(1) Gingivitis is often caused by excessive plaque. It is easy to accumulate between the teeth and the edges of the teeth, and calcification forms calculus. Symptoms are mainly limited to the gums, such as redness, swelling, brushing to bleeding.

(2) Periodontitis often has bleeding, redness, pain, and peeling of the gums from the teeth. It further invades the

alveolar bone and periodontal ligament below the gums, deepens the periodontal capsular bag, causing gum atrophy, root exposure, tooth shake, bad breath, etc. phenomenon.

In the early stage of periodontal disease, there may be only a few redness and swelling of the gums. Once oral hygiene continues to be poor, it may cause serious injury. If the following symptoms appear, the representative may be a warning of periodontal disease:

There are 8 common symptoms of periodontal disease:

1. Bleeding gums when brushing, or bleeding during normal times
2. Bad breath or bad smell in the mouth
3. The gums change from pink to dark red
4. Gingival swelling or pustule formation
5. Gingival atrophy, root exposure and enlarged gap between teeth
6. The teeth are sensitive to cold and heat
7. Loose teeth or chewing weakness
8. The teeth are displaced or unable to mesh properly.

According to statistics from the Ministry of Health and Welfare of Taiwan in 2016, 84.8% of adults over 18 years old in Taiwan have periodontal disease, that is, 10 people, that is, 8 people are troubled by periodontal disease. Taiwan has the highest rate of periodontal disease in Asia. Therefore, the annual medical expenditure of the National Health Insurance Department is 3rd and 4th for dental diseases. The first is 53.316 billion NT for kidney dialysis, and the second is 30.96 billion NT for diabetes. The third place is periodontal disease 18.003 billion NT, and the fourth place is decayed tooth 16.646 billion NT. If the third and fourth places are added up to 180.03+16.46=34.649 billion yuan, dental disease will rank second in the money-burning disease. (Please refer to the A1 front page news of China Times on July 12, 2020) Dr. Li Bojun, Director of National Health Insurance Administration, said in the United Daily News of the 2019.5.12 report: "Preventing periodontal disease, brushing teeth is still the focus", Brushing, that is, cleaning the teeth. But this is only half of the explanation, and did not catch the point.

However, the "old teeth" after the age of 45 form ischemic periodontal disease, which cannot be prevented by only using clean teeth. It is only a cleansing and periodontal disease that has a great cause. The successful cleaning of teeth can prevent dental caries, and dental caries are also one of the important reasons for tooth loss. But brushing one's teeth alone cannot prevent one hundred percent of teeth loss. Therefore, Taiwan forms the Asian region with the highest rate of periodontal disease. The disease that causes the National Health Insurance Agency to burn a lot of money every year, ranked third. The fourth place is dental caries. .

When the tooth falls off, it is the beginning of pain. It will be very tired and painful to eat, and the stomach will be uncomfortable. Because the food is not easy to digest, when you start to spend money, implanting teeth or making dentures is the only two Option, one tooth implant, a good start of 60,000 (N.T), and some people in Taiwan have all implants, all of which cost several million yuan (N.T). To make a denture, you must pay at least 100,000 (N.T), and spend a small amount of money, but these implants and dentures are not as good as your original teeth. Remember, Fake teeth are never better than real teeth. Dental implants also have some shortcomings, please refer to Appendix 5 of P.68 of this book.

Therefore, how to protect your teeth without falling off is a very important thing in Your life. It is a pity that most people have neglected this matter. They all misunderstanding that when they are old, their teeth will naturally fall off, so there is no special care and no scholars to study this matter. In fact, when you are old, you will lose your teeth. It is only a function of blood circulation, which is reduced, and the formation of ischemic periodontal disease can be prevented.

1.2 Eating three meals has a good taste, helps digestion, and prolongs your life.

Humans are animals that eat whole grains. On average, each person needs about 2,000 calories per day. Life can last normally. Therefore, every day, 365 days, you need to use your teeth. When food is chewed by teeth, the mouth will produce. Digesting saliva, making food more delicious, will also enhance your immune system. This is also a kind of enjoyment of life, especially those who pay attention to eating and drinking.

It is also important to note that If you lose a lot of teeth, these enjoyments are gone, your stomach is sometimes uncomfortable because it has no teeth to chew. Human standard teeth, 16 upper and lower, a total of 32. Humans must have at least 20 teeth to have basic chewing function.

Without teeth, it is easy to lose the pursuit of food. It is very important to establish a concept of protecting teeth from falling off from a young age. It is also a kind of psychological construction, a concept of protection. With this concept of protection, your teeth have the hope of keeping them forever. Rather than, let it be, let it go, the misconception that "When I get old, my teeth will fall out naturally." 90% of the world's people have almost the same concept of error. I hope that the school or the relevant units can correct this misconception, Propaganda and Teaching. Can save many people's teeth.

1.3 Speaking will not leak, help you socialize

When your teeth fall off a few times, when you talk, it is often inconvenient, sometimes leaking, and you can't smile normally. It will also cause the reduction of facials, which will cause you a lot of troubles. As long as your teeth don't fall off, these troubles are gone. The teeth do not fall off and the speech is normal.

Based on the above three important reasons, the World Health Organization (WHO) has long announced that 「Dental Health」 is an important cornerstone of general health and quality of life (Please refer to P.72 Appendix 7. World Health

Organization for 9 Important Announcements on "Oral Hygiene")

Western doctors often say: "Healthy teeth, clean mouth, can prevent heart disease and stroke." In patients with severe periodontal disease, the rate of stroke is 1.5 times that of the average person and the cardiac death rate is 2 times.

Dr. Qiu Xianzhong, Director of the Department of Dentistry at the General Hospital of Taiwan's Armed Forces General Hospital, recently stated on the A3 page of the China Times on August 28, 2021: "If you suffer from periodontal disease and get new coronary pneumonia (COVID-19), your risk of death will increase by 8 times. " Therefore, we have to be careful about the relationship between the global pandemic COVID-19 and periodontal disease.

CHAPTER II LITERATURE REVIEW

2.1 Know your teeth and understand the reasons why your teeth can never fall out

Human standard teeth, 16 upper and lower, total 32 (8 incisors, 4 canines, 8 premolars, 12 molars). Humans must have at least 20 teeth for basic chewing. The average length of the teeth is about 1.9-2.3 cm. The visible teeth and gums are only the upper part of the teeth. The teeth stand upright and stand. It relies on periodontal support tissues Such as gums, alveolar bone, and periodontal ligaments to protect the gums. Healthy gums are pale pink. The structure of the teeth is as follows:

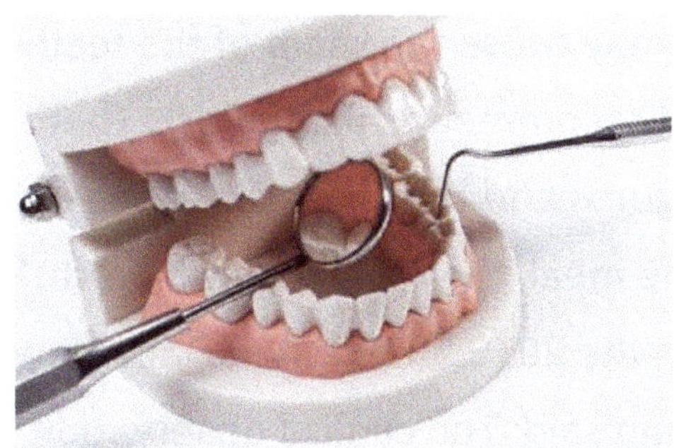

Image 1. Structure of the teeth

There is a hole in the center of the tooth called the "Endodontic pulp." which is filled with nerves, blood vessels and lymphatic vessels, collectively called the pulp. These nerves, blood vessels, and lymphatic vessels are connected to nerves, blood vessels, and lymphatic vessels in the tibia through small holes (apical holes) at the tip of the root. It has the function of forming new ivory and maintaining tooth life.

The cementum is the lateral tissue covering the root of the tooth and has the same structure as the bone marrow, and usually grows for life. When the age is old, the root canal membrane will gradually lose and produce the seam of the teeth. After a long period of time, it will be filled with calculus, it will be filled with tartar for a long time, which is one of the reasons for your tooth loss.

Using a toothpick may cause the seam of the teeth to become larger. The dentist recommends using floss. There is a 2mm depth between the gums and the roots called the "periodontal sac." After the meal, the food slag will be stuffed in the "periodontal sac." In the 2019.5.29 United Daily News D version of the health column said: The clinical observation of Taiwan dentists found: 「That about 90% to 95% of people in Taiwan, the daily way of cleaning teeth is wrong」。

The wrong way of cleaning teeth, that is, easy to cause dental caries (tooth decay), If the tooth decay is serious, and the tooth will be lost after a long time. It is also one of the reasons why humans are prone to tooth loss. Because of this, Taiwan has the highest rate of periodontal disease in Asia.

Therefore, whether the method of brushing your teeth is correct every day is also a very important task for preventing tooth loss. The first chapter explained that people will lose their teeth when their gums are old and form periodontal disease. This chapter explains that dirty teeth can easily cause dental caries (tooth decay) and tooth loss.

2.2 History of Western Medical and Dentistry

Since the British William Harvey (A.D.1578-1657) discovered in A.D.1628, 「The theory of human blood circulation」 has been marked as the beginning of modern Western medicine. Therefore, the development of Western medical is only 392 years of history, nearly 400 years. In 1661, his student Marcello Malpighi used a microscope to verify his theory. In A.D. 1840, the first dental school, the Baltimore

School of Dentistry opened in Baltimore, Maryland, USA. Therefore, the development of dentists has only been 180 years. Because the development of dentists is only 180 years, at present, there is no natural method for studying how to make teeth not fall off in the dental medical literature. This article is the first one to study this related topic. I hope to attract the attention of World human all over the world.

There were many ways to prevent tooth loss in China 1500 years ago. Sun Simiao (A.D. 557~682), the king of medicine in the Tang Dynasty, created three methods for dental care: Interlock teeth, Secrete salivation, and Gingival massage" He also said, "When I get up in the morning, I interlock my teeth 36 times, but my teeth don't fall." However, these methods use the theory of Chinese medicine to keep the teeth from falling out. Because the time is too early, no one has confirmed it, so they have not been published in the literature of Western medicine (because Western medicine has only 392 years of history. Check Page27), so people around the world know Not much.

This article is the first one published in the Western medical literature in the form of an academic paper to prove how to massage the gums theory with Chinese medicine so that your teeth will not fall out. I hope everyone in the world will know that there is such a simple and easy method..

I had it in 1991. The certificate of the Chinese International Acupuncturist has Chinese medical foundation. I hope that someone will continue to research better and cheaper methods to benefit mankind. Like the current dental implants invented in the dentist industry, all implants cost several million yuan (NT). It is true that the patents of the rich are not beneficial to the general population of 70% of the world. Many people have no money at all and go for dental implants. People in backward areas on the earth, let alone.

2.3 Chinese medical method of protecting teeth

The earliest Chinese medical tooth protection technique was developed by Bodhidharma. He is abbreviated as Dharma, also known as Dharma Patriarch. He was a native of South Tianzhu or Persian in West Asia, and was the first ancestor of Chinese Buddhism and Zen. "Bodhi Dharma" is translated into enlightened Buddhism, Bodhi means "enlightenment", and

Bodhidharma's original meaning is "Dharma." He is an authority and teacher of Chinese health sports medicine.

He is also a pioneer in preventive sports medicine in China. Author of Yi Jin Jing and Washing Marrow Sutra is one of the important books of Chinese preventive sports medicine. However, the content of the book is difficult and it is not narrated in Mandarin, and it is not easy for ordinary people to understand without the guidance of a teacher.

During the Southern and Northern Dynasties of China (A.D. 502-557), the Patriarch Bodhidharma came to Liang in the Southern Dynasties of China in 520 AD. About 1500 years ago, Patriarch Bodhidharma retreated on the wall of the Shaolin Temple in the Shaoshi Mountain of the Northern Wei Dynasty for nine years. Xiangtongmo is the creator of Shaolin Temple's martial arts health treasure "Author of Yi Jin Jing, Washing Marrow Sutra" and Shaolin 72 stunts. There are 41 chapters in Yi Jin Jing. It is a book on prevention of sports medicine. It contains methods to prevent tooth loss, but they are all passed on privately from master to disciple. They are taught in oral language, and textbooks are not required. If you want to learn more about Yi Jin Jing, you can go to Songshan Shaolin Temple, Henan Province, China to study, but you need to prepare a tuition first. You may not get handouts or textbooks. Because the teacher is one-to-one oral teaching.

Then about 50 years later, Sun Simiao (AD 557~682), the king of medicine in the Tang Dynasty, also created three methods of dental health care: "tapping, rinsing, and clasping", and put forward the theory of "percussion for 36 times in the morning, but the old teeth will not fall". With these historical records, it is obvious that it is easy to use teeth until they are 100 years old. It's just that no one will confirm it, and no one will sort it out. No one submits articles to medical websites, so not many people study it, so not many people know about it in the world.

Attachment:

However, in Taiwan in 1948, the world's celebrity President Chiang Kai-shek retreated from mainland China to Taiwan and brought nearly 2 million mainlanders (including 600,000 troops) to Taiwan to operate Taiwan. Among these 2 million people, many of them are scholars and teachers who study Yi Jin Jing. These people are currently scattered throughout Taiwan and are over 90 years old on average. They have made great contributions to Taiwan's traditional medicine, such as teacher Li Fengshan, Teacher Zhou Zuoyu, Teacher Cui Jiechen, Teacher Ren Shude, Teacher Cao Yunzhen，Teacher Zheng Fuzhen, Teacher Wu Ningfang --- etc. These traditional medicines have saved many Taiwanese. It also provides a lot of help to my medical knowledge. One of them, Mr. Ren Shude (Chairman of the Chinese Society of Advanced Science), taught me this set of Patriarch Bodhidharma's tooth protection skills to slow down gum aging (please refer to section 4.1 on page P.42 of this book). These traditional medicines have helped many Taiwanese people. Their contribution to Taiwanese medicine is just that no one has done research and sorting out.

Because after Taiwan's recovery in 1948, the Nationalist government only tried its best to develop Western medicine and did not pay much attention to Chinese medicine, leaving Chinese medicine to fend for itself. Therefore, the standard of Western medicine in Taiwan has reached the world level and has been recognized by the world medical community. But don't forget that mainland China has produced a world-class Nobel Prize in Medicine in 2015. The winner is Tu Youyou, a Chinese medicine practitioner from mainland China. The theoretical basis of Chinese medicine in traditional Chinese medicine has also been obtained and has been affirmed by the world medical community. The idea of this book is to massage the gums to get healthy teeth. It is also one of the medical theories of Chinese medicine.

Western medicine practitioners in Taiwan need to change their minds. They should also learn some common knowledge of traditional Chinese medicine, and some concepts of body health and health in China's "Medical Collection, Huangdi Neijing". (醫藥寶典 黃帝內經) Don’ t just treat the disease, and ignore how the body, your own health care, and the highest level of medicine: the best doctor can prevent the patient’ s disease from happening, not treat the disease.” According to statistics from the Ministry of Health and Welfare in Taiwan in 2018, the rate of "cancer" among the western doctors working at the National Taiwan University, the affiliated hospital of the medical school, is more than three times that of the average person in society. Can you not feel distressed? Therefore, the life expectancy of Western medicine practitioners in Taiwan is shorter than that of traditional Chinese medicine practitioners in Taiwan.

Chapter III: Secrets of teeth not falling off

Before I explain the method of the teeth not falling off, everyone must fully understand why your teeth will fall naturally, it is necessary to solve the tooth fall according to the reason of the tooth fall. There is a way to keep your teeth from falling out.

The first and second chapters of this book emphasize the medical theory of why your teeth fall naturally and how to use massage gums to prevent gum aging and prevent teeth from falling naturally.

Note: Before massaging the gums, wash your hands with clean water. If you suffer from periodontal disease, please ask your dentist to cure the periodontal disease. In the three stages, you should concentrate on brushing your teeth and massaging at the beginning of your movements, and develop the habit of not having any distracting thoughts.

3.1 Healthy brushing (Preparation action)

Toothpaste + toothbrush (Time: 3~3.5 minutes)

Use a toothbrush and toothpaste (use mild toothpaste without hurting the skin inside your mouth) and brush your teeth around the front, back, top, bottom, and teeth. Be careful not to use water for a while, and rinse off the toothpaste. The above is normal brushing for 3~5 minutes. Please concentrate on brushing your teeth and don't have other distracting thoughts (please refer to page P.64, Appendix I. How to Brush Healthy Teeth).

Next, massage the gums and massage the gums with the toothpaste on your mouth. Note: If you brush your teeth in the wrong way, using the cutting method will damage the enamel and dentin of the tooth. If the tooth is damaged into the cavity of the tooth wall, Tooth loss can occur when the cave is too large or severe. Ask a dentist as soon as possible to fill up the cave or add a tooth cover. There is no need to pull out the tooth.

3.2 Middle finger massage gum + qigong

After the tooth is brushed, the toothpaste in the mouth is used as a lubricant. The middle finger is used in a very order, and the gums of each tooth are massaged. The gums of each tooth have two sides (front and back), so 32 teeth have 64 faces. The advantage of using the middle finger is that you can massage the gums hard, the size of the force, easy to control by yourself. The gums will be very comfortable, not painful, massage with your finger. Massage with index finger is also possible. Fingers need to be washed first.

Massage your gums with a toothbrush sometimes has a painful feeling, which is less than reachable and a full massage effect. Why not massage with a toothbrush, the reason is here.

Massage on each side of the gums, the width of each massage is about 2 widths of the teeth, first up and down 9 times, left and right each 9 times, each time a total of 18 times, 32 * 2 faces * 18 / 2 (2 groups, massage at the same time) = 576 times, from the first to the 32, do not miss (2 groups of massage at the same time), after 32 is completed, repeat again. It takes about 3 to 5 minutes.

Before washing off the toothpaste with water, massage the gums with your index finger + toothpaste. You must have toothpaste to help the massage to produce the massage effect, otherwise it will be astringent. Toothpaste does not need to spend money, because you originally need toothpaste to clean your teeth every day. Do not miss any gums.

Qigong = (When massaging, Concentrate and meditate on your blood flowing in your gums)

3.3 Massage gums + Qigong + Clear water (Massage while letting water clean the toothpaste)

In the third stage, when the toothpaste is cleaned with water, massage 2 gums at the same time (a group of 2 massages at the same time), first up and down 9 times, left and right each, 9 times, each with a total of 18 drops, 32 capsules *2 side*18/2 (2 pieces in a group)=576 times, after 32 pieces are completed, repeat again. The third stage will take about 3~5 minutes. The above three stages, all of the time, will take at least 9-15 minutes.

Other matters needing attention:

1. The second and third stages of massage gum movements, while having the effect of cleaning teeth (anti-caries). However, in the first stage of cleaning the toothbrush, the method of brush your teeth is very important. If The brushing method is wrong, it will damage the enamel and dentin of the tooth. If the enamel and the dentin of the tooth are damaged, it will become a wall cave & will Lost your teeth.

Before you have lost your teeth, you must ask the dentist to fill the cave. Don't make a decision lightly, just pull out your teeth.

2. The above massages are performed twice in the morning and evening, at least twice a day. After two days, you can see the effect. Be careful to eat anything, be sure to gargle, after eating and three meals, be sure to gargle, Especially, after eating lemon, carbonated drinks, sweets, tea, coffee. You must gargle your mouth with clean water. Gargle is just a matter of effort, but it is a very important daily action, because it can't cause tooth decay. Massage + cleaning teeth + Gargle. This is the recipe for success. It must be done at the same time every day. Bring a kettle with you. You can rinse your mouth at any time to ensure that your teeth are kept clean. Only massage, not clean your teeth, not rinse your mouth, or No, the teeth may be decayed.

Massage + teeth cleaning + gargle is the formula phrase for success. It must be done whole daily to ensure that the teeth do not fall out.

3. When you massage, find that gum bleeding, massage the gums, massage a few times, If it is degenerative gum bleeding, the bleeding may stop and the massage has

achieved the effect. If the gums are not bleeding during the massage process, the teeth that represent that you have normal teeth. However, if you have a serious periodontal disease, please consult a dentist for diagnosis and treatment.

4. Normal gums are not sore when massaged. If you have sore gums, you should massage the gums, because the gums of that tooth are about to become periodontal. For patients with periodontal disease infected with bacteria, you should first ask the dentist to cure the periodontal disease and then perform the gum massage.   The aging phenomenon of gums becomes more obvious with age. Young people, improper use of teeth, or improper protection, gum tissue, it is also easy to attract damage and tooth loss occurs. Pure ischemic periodontal disease, and no bacterial infection, sometimes can be treated with massage gums.

5. To protect teeth from falling out, you should start at a young age, and the sooner the better, because serious tooth decay can also cause young people to lose their teeth. If the tooth decay is serious, you must seek a dentist to remove the tooth.

Chapter IV Results and discussion of gum massage

4.1 Massage gum results

I am 72 years old this year. I was born in Taiwan in 1948. I was born in Dalin Township, Chiayi Hsien. Taiwan R.O.C. when I was 14 years old in 1963. I studied at Douliu Zhengxin Middle School in Yunlin Hsien. I met My teacher Ren Shude. That, He is my junior high school physical education teacher. He also studied the health maintenance skills of Master Bodhidharma .He is 35 years old in 1963. Teacher Ren Shude and President Chiang Kai-shek came to Taiwan together from mainland China in 1948.

When I was 45 years old in 1993. I was in Xinzhuang City, Taipei. I met teacher Ren Shude again. At that time, my gums started to bleed sometimes. When I spoke, there was bloody smell in my mouth. Teacher Ren Shude, who taught me massage gums the method of protecting the teeth, I have been doing dental care every day since then, and by 2020 this year, my teeth are all good, all original.

Of course, I have accumulated 27 years of practical experience (1993~2021) and tests for this set of tooth skills. Proved to be effective, free, simple, and without side effects. It was also taught to many of my close friends, relatives and friends, with good results. Today, in addition to thanking Teacher Ren Shude, for his oral teaching, I would like to use this set of 27 years of experience in protecting the natural health of teeth for the whole world. Everyone knows that if you do the correct gum massage + tooth cleaning + mouthwash, you will be able to protect your teeth to 100 years old and reduce the huge medical cost of the society. It will also reduce your chances of going to the dentist for treatment. After reading the story in this book and following the method, you don’ t have to lose your teeth, implant your teeth, or dentures. You can also make a small profit (currently a dental implant costs at least 60,000 N.T in Taiwan). Why not?

Stick to Persist+Determining to practice this method, you will get unexpected results, because this method is free and has no side effects. The Qian Hexagram of the Book of Change (易經乾卦) tells us that you can only get what you want if you insist on Persist+Determining Determination. To protect teeth from falling out, you must also persist in Persist+ Determination.

4.2 Effective theoretical basis that human teeth will not fall out

The first and second chapters of this book have briefly explained the effective theory of massaging the gums to prevent teeth from falling out. This section discusses in depth again.

Gingival massage can promote the blood circulation of periodontal tissues, strengthen the stable tissue metabolism of the teeth & avoid aging gums, Relatively enhance the ability of teeth stabilization, and prevent the natural loss of teeth.

This is the reason to massage the gums, effectively prevent the teeth from falling off, and the Chinese medical massage acupuncture points, effectively improve the blood circulation function, can treat the disease theory, the theory is consistent with each other, The key is that you must make the right massage method, and you must do it every day without interruption, and massage the gums at least 2 to 3 times a day for 9 to 15 minutes each time to achieve the massage effect. The trick is here. This is the secret of success.

The gum is the base for fixing the teeth, the base is stable and the teeth are not easy to fall. There must be sufficient blood in the gums to prevent the gums from aging. The gums are full of blood vessels. As long as the blood flow in the blood vessels is normal, and the gums are not aging, the tooth base is stable. Therefore, you can rely on massage to normalize the blood flow of your gums to prevent aging of your gums, and your teeth will be stable.

As humans get older, their ability to move blood is deteriorating. The gums will age naturally .Therefore, if you don't do something, the teeth will start to fall out naturally until they are all out (commonly known as, when the human is old, some old people will start to lose their teeth). By allowing the blood flow in your gum vessels to flow normally, you can prevent your teeth from aging and prevent your teeth from falling out.

Please be sure to understand how to massage your gums, why it can stop your teeth and naturally fall off. After understanding the reason, do the method in this book again, the effect will be doubled. Just as you protect your knees, you must understand the cause of your knee injury and protect your knees. This will be easier.

The human mind is very intelligent, so science is also changing with each passing day. Maybe one day, human beings can invent a medicine. After eating, the blood vessels of the gums can flow normally, and the teeth will not fall off. However, before the drug was invented, it was necessary to rely on massage to prevent the tooth from falling off. This method is natural and free. Only nature is the most valuable.

Only by observing the laws of the earth's natural world will the body be healthy. This is also the reason why the United Nations has always asked countries all over the world to save energy and reduce carbon in order to make the planet healthier. Because of a large amount of production of carbon, it has caused the Earth "extreme climate" and intensifier.

4.3 The effect of massage on gums is limited

(In addition to massage, you must add + cleansing + mouthwash, only massage the gums, it can not 100% prevent tooth decay and tooth loss)

Don't think that only massaging the gums is omnipotent. It can only reduce the chance of tooth falling by

70%, but it can't 100% prevent the tooth from loss. Because there are other factors 30% that can make you lose your teeth, such as teeth decay . Because you often eat something every day to replenish your energy, such as snacks, which will stain your teeth and cause tooth decay.

Severe tooth decay will cause you to lose your teeth. This has nothing to do with massaging your gums. It is another cause of tooth loss.

If you eat something, you don't gargle mouth. If you have a long time, you may have a tooth decay. Although you have massaged your gums, your tooth decay may also cause you to lose your teeth. Therefore, in addition to massaging the gums, it is also necessary to develop the habit of cleaning teeth and gargle. Massage、tooth cleaning、and gargle are all indispensable , and they are all very important.

The above massage of gums can only help your teeth, and 70% of them can prevent them from falling out. But your teeth may fall. To keep 100% your teeth from falling, you must rely on your correct method of cleaning your teeth and your mouth-washing habit. After eating and three meals, you must rinse your mouth, especially eating lemons, carbonated drinks, sweets, tea, coffee. Be sure to rinse your mouth.

Therefore, Dr. Xu Zhengzhong from Tainan Annan Hospital put forward that "To prevent periodontal disease, correct teeth cleaning is very important. Three tools for cleaning teeth" please refer to Appendix III. P.66. It is necessary to keep the area around the teeth clean all day long to prevent tooth decay to ensure that the teeth do not fall out.

There is no one way in the world. It is perfect, and people are not perfect. Chinese proverb "The same rice can be made into hundreds of species people" Not necessarily, there will be a few out of a hundred people. Those who are not used to this method are psychologically unable to adapt to finger massage. Some people use their fingers to massage their gums and may feel disgusted in their hearts. But in the medical field, as long as there is a 90% success rate, it is considered effective.

Dr. Li Bojun, Director of the National Health Insurance Administration, said in the Unity Dally News of the 2019.5.12 Vitality column. report: "It is not enough to brush your teeth once in the morning and evening." It is best to carry an interdental brush with everyone. As long as you have finished eating, you will use the interdental brush first. Remove the food inside the teeth and use a small toothbrush to remove the bacteria accumulated in the gums, avoid the formation of calculus, the calculus in the mouth, bad breath will appear over time, and the calculus may cause bleeding of the gums, resulting in periodontal disease. The symptoms of the disease, and finally the teeth are dropped.

Other matters needing attention:

1. Humans have 32 teeth. Due to the wrong way and method of cleaning teeth, it sometimes causes tooth cavities and wall cavities. When a cave is found, the dentist should be taken as soon as possible to fill the cave. If the cave is deep, the depth will reach the nerve. Bringing a big illness.

Fixed time every year, develop habits, dental health check at least once a year, just like a physical health check. "One tooth hurts, the whole body is affected" If the tooth is too corroded, it is best to make a tooth cover to protect the whole tooth to prevent the cave from getting bigger, the teeth continue to deteriorate, and the tooth must be extracted. The tooth cover is relatively cheap, currently about 2,500 (N.T) to 5,500 (N.T) per tooth cover.

According to the World Health Organization (WHO), 60% to 90% of school-age children and nearly 100% of adults worldwide have dental caries . This shows the severity of tooth decay worldwide. Please note that dental caries and tooth decay are also one of the reasons for tooth loss.

2. If the tooth is to fall off, it is a sign. It will not suddenly fall. Its premature period will give you about one to two weeks. The human organs are clever and Almost before getting sick, there is an early warning system. Before you get sick, there will almost always be signs, the length of time, just whether you care about it. For example, the sign of Covid-19 is fever and cough..

There are two signs of tooth loss: The first is that when you brush your teeth, there will be signs of bleeding in the gums, and healthy gums will not bleed. The second is that during the daytime, although the tooth brush is very clean, you will feel your mouth. When talking to people, the mouth is full of bloody stench all day long, with a bloody smell. The person who talks with you feels the deepest and feels uncomfortable, But The person who smells the smell is embarrassed, but he's embarrassed, tell you.

When these signs come, special attention should be paid to the preparation of the teeth to fall off. When the tooth falls off, it is too late to save it. Because adults, teeth fall behind, the teeth can’ t be regenerated. The tooth protection method taught in this book can not only prevent your teeth from falling, but also help you to clean your teeth and reduce your chances of tooth decay. It is a great help for your daily health care. Carry a bottle of water with you at all times. When you have finished eating, you must remember to gargle your mouth or brush your teeth.

3. If you have a problem with your teeth, try to find an experienced and patient dentist, but the dentist can't help you, let the teeth never fall off. Because they can only alleviate, your teeth are ill, to temporarily help your teeth clean and prevent further deterioration, Normal maintenance depends on yourself. To keep your teeth from falling out, you can only rely on yourself to establish a correct concept of tooth protection.

4. Toothpaste must use a mild toothpaste that does not allow the toothpaste to damage the skin in your mouth. Because toothpaste is a lubricant, it can help your fingers, massage the gums, and produce a massage effect. The toothpaste must stay in the mouth for more than ten minutes.

The toothpaste must be mild. After massaging the gums at night, eat again, remember to gargle, so as not to cause tooth decay.

5. Protect your teeth so that your teeth don't fall off. When you see this book, start doing it. Regardless of your age, no matter how many teeth you have now, protecting your existing teeth, as a matter of urgency, follow the third chapter of this book. How many teeth are there, how many teeth are protected. 「Retaining the original tooth is the best dental protection policy」 Never pull out the remaining teeth easily. Instant, there are three teeth left, and it has its function. Don't give up these three teeth easily.

In 2019, in Taiwan, there is an 80-year-old woman surnamed Zheng in the south of Taiwan . She has three teeth in her upper jaw. There are no teeth left in her lower jaw. The director of the Tainan Hospital of the Ministry of Health and Welfare Taiwan, Yao Yizhen, helped her to change her lower jaw to a fixed denture. Active dentures for her upper jaw, Zheng surnamed women laughed and said: "Good use, with dentures, three teeth, but also bite the cartilage and peanuts."

Chapter V Conclusions and Recommendations

5.1 Conclusions :

Teeth can be used up to 100 years old

Based on my 27 years of gum massage protection experience and Chinese medical records over the past dynasties, I wrote this book, how to keep your teeth from falling out? theoretically, it is feasible for human body structure. Will you succeed in protecting your teeth from falling out? It's just whether you have this concern, "I want protect my teeth to never fall out". If you have this protection, you will succeed in protecting your teeth.

If you read this book, get the concept of tooth protection, and practice it, you will surely keep your teeth from falling out. It is very easy thing to use teeth until 100 years old.

And this book, the method of protecting your teeth, is free and simple and has no side effects. For your own healthy teeth, please massage your gums every day, then clean your teeth properly and develop the habit of gargle after eating. These 3 things must be done continuously throughout the day: massage gums + clean teeth + gargle habit. Not only will it bring healthy teeth, but it will bring you an endless future and improve the quality of your life.

Book of Changes: Qian Hexagram.(乾卦) Telling us that "The universe is running in a very normal way. Every day, human beings must work diligently, struggle, and cannot stop." It is right to do the right thing.

5.2 Recommendations: Three suggestions

(Three suggestions 1~3. the remaining 4~7. For reference to WHO & Government officials and medical personnel .)

1. There are many benefits to keeping your teeth from falling, so people must prevent their teeth from falling.

Preventive action is the best method of medicine, Since you see this document, you are blessed, just do it, and go to practice, you will get it, unexpected. effect. Don't wait for tomorrow, just come and do it. Tomorrow, We never know where it is? And the teeth are going to be used for a lifetime. In time, you can't wait.

2. In addition to this book's method of massaging gums, you must clean your teeth correctly every day, and develop the habit of frequent gargle. Remember these three mnemonic formula ， Massage + teeth cleaning + gargle . In this way, you can prevent teeth from falling. Note: Only massage the gums can′ t prevent 100% tooth decay. You must rinse and clean your teeth. Because of the serious tooth decay, the dentist will advise you to remove the tooth. Therefore, to protect teeth from falling out, it should be done at a young age, the sooner the better.

3. Grateful and humble spirit to protect our teeth. Is it effective to massage the gums? After two days, ask yourself, the most correct answer. If it is effective, introduce it to your husband, wife, children, relatives and friends, use this method to protect your teeth and protect your teeth for a lifetime. You will get very healthy teeth. Since childhood, you can't forget how to protect your teeth every day, and you will be happy every day. If you forget it a little, your teeth may fall.

4. According to statistics from the Central Health Insurance Administration Taiwan in 2020 : The number of people with dental disease in Taiwan is 906.1+577.9=1484 ten thousand each year, which is about 37 times (1484/39.7=37

times) the number of people with chronic kidney disease, which is a kind of disease. Very expensive diseases, ranked 3rd and 4th (3rd periodontal disease, 4th dental caries, 1st dialysis disease, 2nd diabetes). Taiwan really has room to improve dental education for the nation's health care. (Refer to P.20 of this book)

5. The theory of massaging gums introduced in this book to protect teeth was put forward in China 1500 years ago. In addition, the Tang Dynasty medicine king Sun Simiao (581~682) also advocated the methods of tooth health care: "Knock, rinse, wipe." It's just that many people in the world (including many Chinese, of course) don't know that there is such a method. No one is going to promote it. This book is the first book to use the theory of Chinese medicine to promote dental health care for the whole people. Moreover, in the 20th century, the Chinese people in the 20th century, due to the corruption of the Qing government and the invasion of China by the world's powers, many Chinese blindly pursued Western medicine, excluding the advantages of Chinese medicine, and would rather pursue Western medicine. However, these concepts of blindly rejecting Chinese medicine, the 2015 World Nobel Prize in Medicine, proved to be wrong.

6. Is there any scientific basis for Chinese medicine? Does Chinese medicine have medical effects? Let' s see, in 2015, the winner of the World Nobel Prize in Medicine was a Chinese physician from Mainland China, Dr. Tu Youyou of Chinese Medicine. Chinese medical theory has been recognized by the world and western medical community.

Some Western doctors and dentists in Taiwan should change these misconceptions. If they have the opportunity, they should learn Chinese medicine to protect themselves and not only treat diseases (please refer to P.35 in this book). There is a doctor of western medicine in Germany (in 2007, he completed his doctorate of western medicine in Germany), Dr. Peter Karl Mayer, Dr. Peter Karl Mayer, who will be 45 years old in 2021 and fell in love with Chinese medicine.

At the age of 31, he completed his degree in Western Medicine in West Germany in 2007 and gave up his high-paying position in Western Medicine in Germany. At the age of 31, he made a special trip to Taiwan to study Chinese medicine at the China Medical University in Taichung City. After 12 years, he has now completed his studies. When he was 43, he had obtained his ID card in Taiwan in 2019. And settled in Taichung

City, Taiwan, and engaged in the work of Chinese medicine practitioners and teaching research.

Can you believe that Chinese medicine also has the advantages of Chinese medicine? Blindly rejecting Chinese medicine will only harm oneself and cannot help patients. The human preventive medicine of China's "Medical Book, Yellow Emperor's Internal Classic" can not only help you cure diseases, but also help you live longer. Many of them are Western medicine textbooks and cannot be learned.

7. The Book of Changes is the wisdom crystallization of 5000 years of Chinese cultural thoughts. People all over the world come to study the Book of Changes, there is no nuclear war in the world

Why do people study the Book of Changes? Anyone who studies the Book of Changes knows that there are 64 hexagrams in the Book of Changes, which teach us 64 principles of life, which can guide everyone to establish a sound concept of life, including how to healthy their own body? Naturally, it includes teeth. There are 3 opportunities in this book, mentioning the close relationship between tooth protection and the Book of Changes.

Among them is a hexagram that teaches all mankind how to coexist peacefully and coexist on the earth. It is the hexagram of Heaven Fire and Mankind. Therefore, in the blood of Chinese people, there is no gene for invading others, being king or dominating. This is because the Book of Changes teaches us the basic principles of life.

The Chinese take the hexagram of Heaven Fire and Mankind of the Book of Changes as a lesson to create the future of the earth, and mankind must continue to build a community with a shared future for mankind. Therefore, peace, harmony, and balance are the ideas and goals that the Chinese have pursued and passed on for more than 5,000 years. Therefore, if China is strong, it will not invade or abuse other countries. Americans must be at ease.

The hexagram of Heaven Fire and Mankind of the Book of Changes is to warn: "Humankind on the earth, mankind must pursue peace on the earth, that is, the pursuit of world harmony and a world where the world is public. Everyone must have the spirit of seeking similarities and differences, and sharing blessings and misfortunes. 』

The Chinese and the Japanese are absolutely different. The Japanese ancestors sent many people to China 1500 years ago, during the Tang Dynasty, to absorb the essence of Chinese culture and technology, and obtain the Chinese Book of Changes, but only learned the book. Half of the story did not fully understand the content, so they attacked Pearl Harbor in the United States in 1941. The Chinese will never do things that hurt the heavens and the truth.

There are some Americans who are worried about China’ s rise and strength, but it’ s actually superfluous., because these people do not understand the Chinese because they have not studied the Book of Changes. There are many misunderstandings for the Chinese. It is mistaken that China, like Japan, will invade other countries if it is strong.

Former U.S. Secretary of State Henry Kissinger , Is one of the people in the United States who knows the Chinese best. He is 97 years old this year in 2021. Recently, on April 25, 2021, he made the most correct & important three suggestions to the U.S. government & Americans :

(1.) China is different from the Soviet Union. The Soviet Union disintegrated and lost to her economy.

(2.) The United States also needs to learn to "coexist with each other" with a big country like China

(3.) The conflict between China and the United States may lead to the end of the world.

The above three suggestions by Henry Kissinger are worthy of careful consideration by all Americans and people all over the world.

References

1.Dharma's ancestors " Change Book Rib " A.D. 520 ～540.

2.''The Method of Thousand Golden Wings'' 「千金翼方 」 Author Chinese Tang Dynasty Sun Simiao A.D. 581~682.

3. Ren Shude Professor, "Chinese National Super medical Introduction" 1993.

4. National Kaohsiung University of Applied Sciences Dr. Lin Zongzeng "Thesis Writing" 2012

5. "Oral Care" Author Zheng Xinzhong . Morning Star Press 2007

6. " Gossip of the Book of Changes"「易經八卦基礎」 by: Professor Xu Yongbai 2019.

7. "Knee Protection" Dr. Lu Shaorui, Director of Department of Orthopedics , Dalin Tzu Chi Hospital, Chiayi Hsien 2020. P.19

8. "The course of periodontal disease is related to the tooth-cleaning habits, and is related to age and bone loss." by Zhou Xinghua, associate professor of

the School of Stomatology, Taipei Medical University 2019. P.19

9. "Preventing periodontal disease, brushing teeth is still the focus" Dr. Li Bojun, Director of Taiwan's National Health Insurance Administration 2019 P.22

10. "Precious Book of Chinese Medicine, the Book of the Yellow Emperor's Internal Classics" By Dr. Fernando Liu Xianping 「中國醫藥寶典，黃帝內經」2020 P.34

11. " Bass brushing Technique" by the American Dental Association P.65

12. "Oral Health" by World Health Organization WHO P.72

Appendix

The following Appendix 1.~6 , because each person's preferences are different, for reference only, if there is any problem during operation, The Dentist & Chinese Doctor should be consulted, but the principle is unchanged.

Appendix 7 WHO information is absolutely worth it, the rules of tooth protection you refer to and abide by.

1. Healthy brushing of teeth

Use a toothbrush and toothpaste to clean and clean each side of your teeth. Note (the toothbrush can be about 2 teeth width, the upper and lower brush counts 6 times), The direction of the toothbrush can only be brushed up and down, not left and right, and no force is required. The left and right brush is called cutting, easy to destroy the tooth enamel, forming a wall hole. In the flat place of the caries, use a round wipe in the original place, and wipe off the dirt, no need to use force. How about the order of brushing, it doesn't matter, you are used to it, you can't forget that it hasn't been brushed yet.

Repeat the above actions at least twice. The toothbrush uses a soft brush, which is at a 45 degree angle to the gingival sulcus, especially at the intersection of the gums and the teeth. Which likely to cause stones. After the stone, it is not easy to clean.

. When brushing your teeth, in front of the mirror with sufficient light, open your mouth and brush your teeth, and see the teeth as clearly as possible to ensure that each side has a brush. The above is normal, normal brushing, time is about 3 to 5 minutes.

A washed toothbrush can be soaked in salt water in a cup. A toothbrush soaked in salt water is helpful for tooth protection, and the toothbrush will not produce germs. The brine should be replaced once a week.

2. "Bass brushing Technique" Recommended by The American Dental Association

(1) The toothbrush bristles are at 45 degrees to the teeth and cover the teeth and gums.

(2) Two teeth and two brushes, the toothbrush

has about 2 teeth width.

(3) The toothbrush goes up and down and back and forth. Count the number up and down 6 and repeat it again after the completion.

3. Three tools for cleaning teeth (1) Soft toothbrush (2) Interdental brush (3) Floss

(1) Soft toothbrushes, choose a soft brush and brush gently.

(2) Interdental brush, brush between the teeth, one size smaller than your own teeth.

(3) Floss, can' t be used too much force, the floss is attached to the teeth, showing a C-shape, and a tooth gap should be cleared twice.

4. How do you know that your teeth have been cleaned?

In the 2019.5.29 United Daily News reported D version of the health column said: Taiwan dentists clinical observation found that about 90% to 95% of Taiwanese people, the daily way of cleaning teeth is wrong. because of this, there are many patients with periodontal disease and dental caries in Taiwan, and the Taiwan National Health Insurance Agency squeezed into money-burning diseases in 2019, ranking third and fourth. (Please refer to P.22 of this book)

So you must know, is your teeth cleaned? How do you know if your teeth are brushed dry?

After brushing your teeth, use a red liquid (CHROMO-T-RED) display solution, available at the general dentist's office. Apply a cotton stick to the red display solution and apply it to the washed teeth. If it is washed, the red display liquid will turn pale. Can't stick to the teeth. If it is not cleaned, the red display solution will become stuck in a place where the teeth are not clean and become red and dark. So you can judge whether you brush your teeth or not, and brush your teeth is not successful. Each time you brush your teeth, you can repeat the test with red liquid until the brush is clean.

When you repeatedly use the red display liquid to detect, in the process, you will be understood, get the essentials and skills of brushing. These essentials and techniques should be kept in mind, and there is no need to show display liquids in the future. But every six months, it is best to use red display liquid to check once, to see if your brushing method, there is no regression or progress.

5. Review of dental implant technology history

A review of the medical history of dental implants. Dental implants were initiated by the Swedish scholar professor Pi-Ingvar-Brenmark in 1952. Titanium metal can be used for the restoration of human bones.

However, in 2012, a 30-year dental implant study by Taiwanese dentist Lin Taiwu published an international revolutionary review report: "After dental implants, there are many shortcomings, and there are better ways to replace dental implants. That is, clip teeth." Please refer to You-tube, dentist Lin Taiwu, or Dongsen Financial News meets big shots. The results of this research have been on the stage of international dentistry in the world, and have been valued by some dentists in the Soviet Union and the United States.

6. Chinese medicine in the past, dental health care methods

(1) Chinese medicine emphasizes that "teeth are leftovers of bone, leftovers of kidneys, and gums are meridians of the stomach." Chinese medical refers to periodontal disease as tooth yaxuan (牙宣), When there is a problem with the gums , the toothbrush bleeds. It is periodontal disease.

Gum is also one of the basis for inspection by Chinese physicians. "Gum is the collateral of the stomach". The upper row of teeth gums is located in the meridian line of the Foot Yangming Stomach Meridian, and the lower row of teeth gums is located in the meridian line of the Hand Yangming large intestine meridian. Chinese medicine Gan Lu Yin, & Yunu Fried decoction,「甘露飲」，「玉女煎」can alleviate the swelling and pain of gums.

Usually pay attention to a balanced diet. Mung beans, loofah, watermelon, celery, pear, mulberry, kiwi fruit, etc. all contribute to gum health. The elderly should pay attention to bone loss. Calcium should be supplemented and sun exposure for at least 15 minutes a day.

(2) The tongue is in the gingival rotation method, This method was founded by Master Bodhidharma about 1500 years ago.

The tongue is on the gums, rotate 360 degrees clockwise and counterclockwise, each 36 times, when the action, if saliva is produced, that is, the intention is to swallow the saliva to the position of the Dantian 「丹田」acupoints. This method can not only strengthen the heart function, but also It can also strengthen the tooth base and strengthen the body's immune system. Human saliva contains many immunoglobulins, amino acids, enzymes, and calcium, which can recalcify teeth.

(3) When urinating or defecate , touch the toes on the ground, and the upper and lower teeth bite each other tightly (when urinating, it is best to stepping with both feet at the same time). The brain's mind blood circulates between the upper and lower gums. When the urination is completed, loosen Upper and lower teeth, about 1 to 5 minutes each time. This method can strengthen the gum tissue and prevent premature aging of the gums. According to the study of Western Medical Urology, human beings drink at least 2000 c.c.

of water a day, urinate 8-10 times, and defecate at least once a day.

(4) Clicking the teeth method, after three meals, clicking the teeth can strengthen the kidney and healthy spleen, and help digestion. Do not tap too much force, so as not to damage the tooth tissue. This is the book "The Method of Thousand Golden Wings" 「千金翼方」by Chinese physician Sun Simiao from A.D581~682 of the Tang Dynasty.

(5) In the Qing Dynasty, the Chinese Physician Chen Xiuyuan (A.D. 1753~1823) used a prescription for strengthening teeth (grinded into powder from nine kinds of herbs) 「固齒神方」. It is suitable for dental health care and has the functions of disinfecting, relieving pain and strengthening teeth.

(6) Modern, Mr. Zhang Butao (former Executive Yuan, Chairman of the Chinese Medicine Management Committee) "Rhizoma Drynariae," 「骨碎補」can treat toothache, has the effects of invigorating the kidney, strengthening bones and relieving pain.

7. WHO World Health Organization's 9 Important Announcements on "Oral Hygiene"

WHO have announcement:

Every March 20th is "World Oral Health Day". Every September 20th is "International Day for Teeth Care"

*The following announcement documents are very important to people all over the world

(1.) Teeth are an important cornerstone of general health and quality of life.

(2.) 95% of the main causes of human tooth loss are caused by periodontal disease and dental caries . That is to prevent the occurrence of periodontal disease and dental caries, it can prevent 95% of the tooth loss.

(3.) Natural teeth appear completely off, and about 30% (65-74 years old) of the world do not have natural teeth.

(4.) 15% to 20% of the world's middle age (35 to 44 years old) suffer from periodontal disease that causes tooth loss.

(5.) Worldwide (60% to 90%) school-age children and nearly 100% of adults have caries. This shows the severity of tooth decay.

(6.) In the oral cavity, keep a low concentration of live fluoride to prevent dental caries (tooth decay).

(7.) Smoking cessation and alcohol reduction, can reduce oral cancer, periodontal disease and tooth loss.

(8.) Reduce the amount of sugar intake, balance food nutrition, prevent premature detachment of dental caries and teeth.

(9.) Avoid cheek injuries and heavy blows, reduce the risk of facial damage, prevent trauma and let the teeth fall off.

COPYRIGHT PAGE

How to use your teeth until 100 years old

Publisher: George Ho

Email: hth333249@gmail.com

Author: George Ho

Publication Date: 2020.09.19

Second edition: 2021.9.21

Facebook: https://www.facebook.com/healthteeth.ho

ISBN :978-957-43-7203-4 (Paper Book)

ISBN :978-957-438-111-1 (EPUB)

Price : U.SD 7 (paper-book)

U.SD 5 (e-book)

E-book design and production:

Design and production: George Ho

E-book: playback information: Amozon

File format: Amozon Kindle Create

Thanks to Freepik for providing free pictures of 6525. P.27 Image 1. Free pictures, Thanks to Tabitha Tumer from Unsplash for providing free pictures , and Tanks to Photo Ac for providing free pictures of 841688. Introduction to the inner page & on the cover.

本書中文版 (Chinese Version) : 如何讓牙齒使用到 100 歲

ISBN: 978-957-43-6900-3　(中文紙本書)

ISBN: 978-957-438-080-0　(EPUB 中文電子書)

中文電子書播放資訊

展售處: Readmoo 讀墨 電子書服務平台

網址: http//ebok.readmoo.com.tw

About the Author: George Ho

Author's brief introduction: born 1948

1.Graduated from the Department of Civil Engineering,

Tamkang University 1972

2.Master Bodhidharma, Study Class of Yi Jin Jing 1981

3.Passed the B-level exam for the International Acupuncturist

in Beijing, China 1991

4.National Kaohsiung University of Applied Sciences Disaster

Prevention Research Institute Master 2013

I like to live to be old and learn to be old, and hope that human beings will be healthier and better. Lifelong learning 2021

Medical research work:

1. Secrets of Qigong for preventing stroke Copyright registration by the Ministry of the Interior 8401548 1994.11
2. How to Effectively Succeed in National Health Insurance 1995
3. Do you want to normalize blood pressure healthily and quickly 1996.6
4. The most effective and convenient way to prevent cancer and prevent kidney dialysis 2006.12
5. The cause of cancer has nothing to do with luck, you yourself are the biggest manipulator ISBN: 987-957-43-2393-7 2115.3

Even if you are busy, read this book. i-teeth The best way for humans to protect Your teeth Chinese Medical, Method of protecting teeth

After reading this book, you don't have to lose your any teeth, you don't have to plant your teeth, you don't have to make fake teeth.

After massage your teeth it can reduce your chances of going to the dentist for treatment, and you will never regret it. Save it all, and further improve your quality of life, only cost 7 US dollars.

You will be grateful all your life, you have encountered this book, a book that is very useful.

www.ingramcontent.com/pod-product-compliance
Ingram Content Group UK Ltd.
Pitfield, Milton Keynes, MK11 3LW, UK
UKHW021839270726
14058UKWH00002B/234

9 789574 381111